Mz N: the serial

Mau–reen N. McLane

Farrar Straus Giroux : New York

Mz N: the serial

A Poem-in-Episodes

(not/a novel)

(not/a memoir)

(not/a lyric)

Farrar, Straus and Giroux
18 West 18th Street, New York 10011

Library of Congress Cataloging-in-Publication Data
Names: McLane, Maureen N., author.
Title: Mz N: the serial : a poem-in-episodes / Maureen N. McLane.
Description: First edition. | New York : Farrar, Straus and Giroux,
   2016.
Identifiers: LCCN 2015035377 | ISBN 9780374218874 (hardback) |
   ISBN 9780374714796 (e-book)
Subjects: | BISAC: POETRY / American / General.
Classification: LCC PS3613.C5687 A6 2016 | DDC 811/.6—dc23
LC record available at http://lccn.loc.gov/2015035377

Designed by Quemadura

Our books may be purchased in bulk for promotional,
educational, or business use. Please contact your local
bookseller or the Macmillan Corporate and Premium Sales
Department at 1-800-221-7945, extension 5442, or by
e-mail at MacmillanSpecialMarkets@macmillan.com.

www.fsgbooks.com
www.twitter.com/fsgbooks
www.facebook.com/fsgbooks

10 9 8 7 6 5 4 3 2 1

. . . life . . . a continual allegory . . .

John Keats, letter to George and Georgiana Keats,
14 February–3 May, 1819

What I'm saying now isn't said by me.

Osip Mandelstam, "He Who Finds a Horseshoe"

Identity always worries me and memory and eternity.

Gertrude Stein, *Everybody's Autobiography*

. . . an Episodic person in whom a form-finding tendency
is stimulated precisely by lack of a Diachronic outlook . . .

Galen Strawson, "Against Narrativity"

Experience is a hoax.

Alice Notley, "Experience"

Please improve these pages, benevolent reader, that could
make me more fit to have been here.

Marianne Moore, handwritten inscription
in *The Marianne Moore Reader*

Contents

I

PROEM: Mz N Contemporary   3

Mz N Nothing   11

Mz N Triumph of Life   13

Mz N Growth of a Poet's Mind   16

Mz N History of Philosophy   25

Mz N Evil   34

Mz N Highschool Boyfriend   39

Mz N No Permanent Mind   44

Mz N Enough   51

II

*Mz N Goodbye Hello / Mz N Considers
the Years and the Centuries*   57

Mz N Monster   59

Mz N Hater   63

Mz N Hermit   **65**

Mz N Woman   **70**

Mz N Song   **73**

Mz N River Interval   **74**

Mz N Thirteenth Floor   **76**

Mz N Trans   **82**

Mz N Therapy   **87**

Mz N Baby   **95**

Mz N Calling   **100**

Mz N What   **102**

Mz N Abyme   **103**

Mz N Love Lies Sleeping / Moon   **106**

Mz N Meadow   **108**

Mz N Palinode   **110**

Envoi / N-Voi   **115**

Acknowledgments   **117**

—N—

PROEM:
Mz N Contemporary

Mz N tries
each day very hard
to be contemporary
One must be
absolutely
contemporary
they've harangued
her for over
a hundred years
& who is she
to object?
She admires
after all
beyond Rimbaud
Yvonne Rainer
who in an interview
somewhere sd something like
I am so happy
to have been able to be

contemporary
or was it she was happy
to have made an art
wholly contemporary?
Well.
You're too young
to think so much
Yvonne sd
to Mz N
about death
Mz N felt oddly
abashed but what to do
You thought
whatever you thought
about. That's an evasion
the cognitive therapists
could flush out
of Mz N very swiftly
with their meta-mind techniques
and surely Zen Buddhists
and their American epigones would also say
let the thought pass through
just observe the thought as it passes
That was one
of many mistakes

4

Mz N kept making she held on
to a thought
as to the sharp end
of a knife
which puts her in mind
of an old Setswana proverb
Ellen Kuzwayo taught her
Mmangoana o tshwara thipa ka fa bogaleng
the child's mother grabs
the sharp end of the knife
but Mz N was not a good
enough mother to her thoughts
They raged and sliced
her barely surviving for years until
they didn't. A thought
isn't irrevocable
Arendt sd   Only action
Mz N would take action
against her thoughts
You think
too much her sister
sd which meant
why don't you
chill out?
Why

not?
Mz N
was no riot grrrl
there was no club
she could join to align
herself with weird sisters
or brothers. The three
punkish kids in high school
were heroes
in her private pantheon
but they like odd gods
were remote
as a loon calling
from a far Adirondack
lake. O there's a loon
on the lake I look at
right here right now
Now I am being contemporary
I can bring the now
right into this poem
& when I say
as I now do
with how sad steps
o moon thou climb'st the skies
I am still very contemporary

which is to say

I am alive

as long as this poem

I & the loon & the moon are alive

All the artists

Mz N knows

who are alive want to be

contemporary

It takes effort

to be contemporary

simply being alive

doesn't cut it

One artist made a piece

This Is So Contemporary

which is elegant

and funny like him Tino

Sehgal a piece both contemporary

and a critique

of the enforcement of the law

of the soon-to-be-obsolete

now which consumer

culture and deep structural

forces of finance capital

sustain or so Mz N's been told

—O tempora O mores!
Dance and political economy
and game theory are intricate
choreographies of the now
Critique is dead
Poetry is dead
Tino told her
no one in Europe reads books
It is contemporary
to ironize the contemporary
but in a light way
no one bothers
anymore with the past
There is no longer an Oedipal
pathos or rage to fuel the now
sprung from the paternal then
Sometimes depth
is just depth
Brecht sd
to Benjamin when depth
was still an option
Mz N's deep
inwardness
is positively
German an unfashionable

Innerlichkeit
best cordoned off
in the foreign
dead field of lyric
Inwardness
an effect of repression
but hey
Don't fence me in!
the little dogie
of Mz N's soul
cried to the postmodern
cowboys lassoing
up the language
of reference & branding
it for sale
Sometimes Mz N even feels
conceptual
What is a concept
What is a conceptual artist
An artist
with a concept
Some days
one can't help being Horace
& writing
an ars poetica

9

All day
Mz N has been eating cherries
of a kind she first saw
in Cambridge 1989ish
when her friend Polly
with higher standards for fruit and men
and clothes went to the beautiful shop
on Huron Avenue and bought
these golden cherries
I now eat
as my memory is the fact
of my being alive
& her & you too
& the cherry ripe
I gave my love and that stone
I gave my love still ring
that song that cherry song
still ripe in our live mouths

Mz N Nothing

This is a tale
about nothing
Let's pretend
we have to establish
the scene & characters though movies
do it so much better
to the despair of the novelizing tribe
But let's say
the midafternoon sun
is striking the leaves in the woods
visible from a screened porch
such that the maples liquefy
into a queer green flame.
In the foreground
are ferns, a few daisies,
a black-eyed Susan
or two. Mz N regrets
what she drank
almost as much as what she said.

And then there's what
she didn't do—kiss
for example
the lithe lovely
in the purple sheath that hugged her ass
like the plumskin the plum.
She bites
the plum in her lunch
a lunch someone else
made. Further chapters
will unfold the full ecosystem
of labor and erotics
that structure the whole panoply
of exchanges
that make up "life"
which is the contract
I make with you reader
hungry as we are for the fruit
of the real

Mz N Triumph of Life

Some are alive
easy and slip
into the world's skin
as their own and plums'
Mz N isn't one
or wasn't
Then what is life?
I cried
cried Shelley
in one version
of "The Triumph of Life"
the title of which from one angle
is a satirical title
triumphs in those days
like Romans'
a chance to parade
the victims   in this case
the victims of life

which are in the end
from a mortal angle
everyone
Better never to have been
the old sage said
and each world
rediscovers
No river
No river twice
and yet it seems the same river
however
much you are not the same

He's not so bleak
that sleek and laughing
vegetarian poet

O could you not learn
to swim you idiot
singing yourself
aboard ships
you could sail
but not sail home

Just like you
to learn to sail
and not to swim

Just like Mz N
to dive in
after him

Mz N Growth of a Poet's Mind

Like all children Mz N lived
in archaic
mythic zones
and all the neighbors and kin played their parts to a T
although they never were able to tell her
the whole story.

§

The child Mz N sat on her bed
and wondered: that tree
outside her window
shifted
when her eye
shifted. What to make
of that?

§

16

Mz N and her siblings
had a dog for some time.
They went on vacation &
when they came back
no dog.
They asked the parents:
the dog?
who replied:
what dog?
And some people wonder
why others distrust the obvious.

§

One year Mz N began her great project
of investigative
touch. Like everything
it came about
through reading
and happenstance. Mz N had a friend
who said I do it and then
I worry
what if my roommate
hears?
What if?

Mz N wondered
went home
and discovered a new octave.

§

Mz N sometimes thinks
what N stands for: Nothing.
One day she said
nīhilism
in school & the teacher
paused, chalk between her fingers
like her longed-for cigarette.
What's nīhilism
Another student said I thought
it was *neehilism*.
This was another example
of Mz N bringing up topics
that went Nowhere.

§

the blackest black
is not so black
it cannot take
a blacker black

so Mz N thinks
the void would speak
if void could speak
or of color think

§

Mz N is writing what she hopes will be
a masterpiece: *Mispronunciation:*
the definitive
autobiography. She only includes
the bloopers she remembers.
She is very strict that way.
What's **vá**-gi-na
—hard *g*—
she called to her parents
age five
when they'd plopped her on the sofa
with a picture book
to help her learn
where babies. Some years later she told a story
at dinner
about being very angry
with a persecuting
teacher. I spoke
she sd

with great ve-**hé**-mence.
Her father laughed
a somewhat unkind laugh
and asked her to repeat it.
She did & once again
he laughed.
Mz N vehemently
objects to the making fun of children
who struggle every day
to get their words
and bodies aligned

§

one day after sex
in a century of bad sex
the other one asked Mz N
did I leave you
on the edge
never having had an orgasm
as far as she knew
she sd
quite definitively
no
how would she know

such an edge
are you sure
the other persisted
Mz N thought again
she could say
quite definitively
o yes here I am on the edge
where you left me
the edge
of a certain
abyss
but this
she knew was the answer
to a question
no one was asking

§

Mz N embarks one day upon a sonnet
attracted by the knowledge that it's dead
extinct like dinosaur dodo or bonnet
long replaced by baseball caps on heads

that centuries ago were piled with curls
birds powder wires and such machinery

'twould blow the minds of tattooed boys and girls
who cruise the streets of this new century

Mz N concedes she's antiquarian
old hat old news—"hoarder of ancient dirt"
to quote the mouldy Scot John Pinkerton
but from her dead-end path she won't divert

the airplane made the train a living fossil
relict herself she listens for its whistle

§

Wordsworth never took a plane
but Mz N takes a plane with Wordsworth
on her mind
and other matters: love,
fear, a wish
to die.
Wordsworth had a very sturdy mind
and legs that took him far
into the mountains,
Scottish glens, German
towns and yes across
the Alps. Mz N has never seen

the Alps nor Snowdon
nor a mountain
anywhere beyond the ancient
Adirondacks Wordsworth too she thinks
would like their worndown humps
their pathless woods the rowboats by the shores
of placid lakes ready
for exploring. Young Wordsworth stole
a rowboat
rowed out on a lake one night and found himself
appalled
the mountain strode sublime
after him
and he trembled and his mind
as Burke had said it would
before sublimity
near failed. There are passages
in life
in Wordsworth
he called spots
of time and Mz N has some spots
she sometimes
recollects. But now
she's happy incredulous
in love

and in strange anguish
wants to recollect
nothing. *If it were now*
to die
'twere now to be most happy
she murmurs
with the engine
nearly exploding
with the fragility
and perverse strength of all that lives
and moves and has its being
in the air on the ground in the sea.
Having reached a floating state
of grace, surprised
by joy
she wants to die
life
can only get worse
the mountain
receding below them as they climb

24

Mz N History of Philosophy

Some are fated
to live out the history
of philosophy in their sex life.
In the cave
of illusion Mz N sensed
the realm of pure
ideas elsewhere
immanent in the sky
she would see only once
she'd left the cave and felt
the sun burn her eyes
into truth. Few
can bear
this truth
said Plato brilliant
monster and everyone
philosopher or no
makes her way
back into the cave

enlightened
or not. For her
there were no ideal forms
no ideal table
which all mere tables
could but imitate—
a real
behind the screen
of the real—
There was this god thing
He was personal
She took it personally
as if she were a Calvinist
or capitalist
and salvation and all profit depended
on her alone
her faith alone but faith
in what. Credo
in unum deum
for a long while and then

no credo. Mz N
recapitulated the Reformation
and Counter-Reformation
and several previous
minor and major heresies

in her soul inquiries & agonies years
seven to fourteen
as she would years later discover
through reading
—seven the age of reason
sd the ancients
or was it Shakespeare's Jaques
or was it eleven in Augustine—
They are always trying to fix
reason and the age of reason
so one could consent
to be reasonable about things
one was supposed to be reasonable about—
& one can't help but reason
said genial David Hume—
no other reason!
She would have
being Catholic
a confirmation
She'd be confirmed
if she'd be confirmed
in her faith. Kierkegaard
brought doubt into the heart
of faith though it had coiled there
a long while

not least in those anguished
souls who unsure
of their salvation
in the seventeenth century
drowned themselves.
Look into thy heart
All the historical things
may have happened
but they happen
specifically
to you
a most historical
unpoetical
thing.
A family
can create a world
sustained by other
institutions
can weave a weft
and warp of world
no other air
can penetrate
a while. Only a while
The thing
about the mind

it tunes itself
to secret strings vibrating
elsewhere. If elsewhere
another thing's ringing
or waving or wavering the mind
plucks it out
framing a harp and harpist
out of alien air and singing strings.
The grandfather died
and then the other grandfather
leaving the fatherless parents
flattened.
Where is he
& where is he
I suppose you are going
to tell me
he's gone to heaven
skepticism
a native faculty
of even a four-year-old mind.
They told her
he'd gone to heaven
with the other one.
They uneasily remember
this sometimes the pestering

long-gone child
who can question
without authority
Suffer
the children and suffer
the parents
What is the grass
I think it is the ancient hair
of graves
I think it is the lawn
the twentieth century unrolled
over America
It is a weed that sucks dry the water table
& the grass is the wind in the grass
a green handkerchief
dropped by an absconded god

§

Mz N can think herself
a blank slate
generating a world
out of sense impressions
but for the fact she feels
so uncertainly

she can't trust her senses
Are there five
Are there eight
The humans have devised
so many systems for sensing
and extra-sensing and taxonomizing
Anyone
who awaited stigmata
is a queer empiricist
Mock on mock on
Voltaire Rousseau
And when in a frat house
at fifteen
with a hapless drunk man
a boy really but large
technically and legally a man
how could she know
if he stuck it in
Wouldn't she have felt it
Wouldn't there have been blood
the palpable
something
Wouldn't there have been
as the novels and movies and daytime dramas insisted
blood?

Wouldn't there have been?
not to mention pain
There was nothing
a big fat nothing
Shakespeare's nothing
is a big fat thing
worth killing for
Hero
is a heroine of nothing
Voices drifted
up through a small
window open
a crack the older girls
singing *don't do*
don't do anything
your mother wouldn't want
you to   Her mother
wouldn't want
her to and that's enough
for her to want to
A perfect oppositional logic
of an already enclosed field
of desire.
But what happened?
Whatever happens?

History is what happened
Poetry what could happen
The probability
is they'd fucked
or she'd been fucked
or he'd fucked her
or even in a wild unlikely construction
though one must in strictness admit it
she'd fucked him
And yet
She never really knew
what happened
And there was really no one
around to ask
This
was one of many episodes
in which Mz N had little grasp
of events
much less plot
Why not say what happened?
Why not say
what happened?
What happened?

Mz N Evil

The problem of evil
can be brought home
in a classroom
or a playground
acquiring the shape
of a casually crushed frog
the boys laugh at.
It is not a masculine problem
It is a human problem
And yet some persist
in thinking
the world good
It's not the world's fault
It's you human
Does the lion worry
Does the ox laugh
It is everywhere
a dark spot secretly
rotting the apple

of the soul you gnaw on daily
Autophage Autophage
Ugolinoing your damned self
so intense the baleful pleasures
the little masturbations
the squished life
caught in the grip
of the necessary thrust and thirst
For what else
Was it for this
Who made the world
Who made god
Who made you
What are you
Are you putting on
lipgloss   Are you   Did you
Where are your gym shorts
Why are you late to class
You did what   You borrowed
from another girl   That's dirty
Do you know how foul
There is a line
There is a line you do not
There is a line
of questioning

There is a lining up
at the noonday bell
to go out to the schoolyard
and its games benign
or vicious like children
in all the worlds
Smear the queer
we'd play unselfconscious
Some say
it's about sex
the hateful female
netherworld hellscape
still boiling
the 20th into the 21st century
the rancid suet
of it put out for carrion birds
So jump the rope
& hop the cracks
& break our mothers'
mothers' backs.
Mother of God
Pray for us sinners now
& at the hour of our death.
Mz N is the most blatant
conformist would hiss

before others hissed
would catch the gist
of any teacher's turn
of wrist or phrase sifting
that day's mood or rank
To have no rank or station
To be of no nation
To know an elaborate taxonomy of sin
It was all wrong
Evil is here
but/and elsewhere
not where the cracked nun thinks
she so kind
to the kindergarteners
They haven't yet grown
the second skin
of late childhood
They don't emit
the rank teen stench
that poisons the air
she's so helplessly breathing
when she smacks the hot girl
for sassing & later gets Mz N up
against the blackboard alone
tight lips breathing hot inches

away O the small village inquisitions
local Torquemada O they are hateful
the insurgent girls with their devil-
may-care feathered hair
It's not that you're evil
but it was Mz N knew

MZ N Highschool Boyfriend

There was a highschool
boyfriend there is always
one in young adult
novels since romance is outsourced
to the teens
as in Shakespeare
Mz N was no romantic
about this
very nice highschool boyfriend
she would have said
he was "very nice"
& the parents more or less
approved he seemed nice
undebauched sanitized etc
Mz N was vaguely
excited by the sex
thing which wasn't much happening
& this was irritating
but may have kept her just this side
of launching the chain reaction

& meltdown which would turn her soul
into Chernobyl
Mz N was a catastrophist
which was in her view
the highest realism
This is not the time
to retail the horrors
and pleasures of suburbia
so many
of both & you know them
from so many novels and movies
Mz N had never seen
It seemed overdetermined
to live in a town
named for a famous
lost civilization
Minoa was archaic
then & now the bull
moved his brute force
through her
dreams & she'd ride him
The boyfriend
was conspicuously
nice which was just what she wanted
& not. She was split

that way typical
split the good
daughter raging a beast
within. And so.
The boyfriend
was part of her cover
the elaborate impersonation
of an American teenager
almost everyone engaged in
a vast communal experiment
which led
for white people to consequences
& sociological reflection & TV series
She couldn't see
the boyfriend she could sense
him sort of
nothing clear
She was too much
in her own way
not to mention the boyfriend's
and the crazed mirror
of her self-absorption
intervened a veritable Versailles
of ostentatious non-encounter
in plexiglassed and lockered halls

He was a good
enough boyfriend
for a while
&/so in an experimental
spirit one day
she sd I love you
She didn't
and she didn't
quite not.
It was a thing
to try
out the fatal
banal words
a paradigm
shift so they sd
Nothing
shifted but the deep
tectonic plates that constitute the crust
of her
core shifted
in a spasm
of self-disgust
She didn't feel
it & she didn't not
Why say anything

I heard words
and words full
of holes
aching
Words
are deeds
True and False
Truth or Dare
her tongue
her self
a forked
unknowing thing
that sang two parts
unharmonizing
Even then she saw
the decent boy
with a queer
remoteness
He wasn't up
for her project
of violent self
formation
& soon faded
into the unfinished basement
of her mind

Mz N No Permanent Mind

The great thing
is not having
a mind Mz N read
many years after
she'd acquired
a somewhat permanent
mind. She had a theory
about this situation
inchoate for some years
but which she called in retrospect
and retroactively
"No permanent mind
condition" which was
her condition

How could anyone think
they persisted
in time
& over?
How did anyone know

anything they knew
would be what they knew
tomorrow?
These
were the imponderables
she pondered or was brought to
by "experience"
a noun she didn't believe in
Was this condition
brought on by a crack
in the mind-
brain continuum?
Was it a function
of inadequate parenting some undone
mirroring somehow the world breeding
a lack of faith
in the ongoingness
of self & world?
Was it
she was too sensitive
as the chorus insisted
This is not the same thing
This was a mental
thing with emotional
implications. Since she was a stranger

to herself at any moment
everything it seemed passed
right through her nothing stayed
there was no there
there in the there
of her mind
For
example
she changed schools
several times in crucial years
the pre- and teen
years when the carnival
of thinking and feeling
one's way into whatever
was in full swing.
She knew nothing
most especially the things
she once knew. Each time
she ventured
into a new classroom she greeted
the new world
naked, stripped
of certainty the Tilt-a-Whirl unhinged
from its frame
the lurid requirement

of socialization and piano lessons
facing her a sicko clownface
HAHAHAHAHA FUCK YOU
Everyone tells stories
of how they became X or Y thing
identity identity
what was identity
it seemed a fragile thing
to be
& brittle the chains
identity
She could not escape
the predicament
of being one
among other ones but sometimes
it could be sung
into an elsewhere of co-being
This was chorus
The chorus
comments on the action
& sometimes partakes.
Chorus
presupposes a chosen submission
to the fusion
of co-created sound

Out of many one

or many as the case may be

It would have been useful

if the chorus were Greek and they'd been consulted

or at least asked to respond

to the actions

of the main actors.

Who were the main actors?

Most people

feel themselves

to be some kind of actor even Mrs. Ramsay

though she acts

more as a stage manager

invisible-handing the courtships along

and soothing the Mister

is an actor

Her knitting is a deep action

Children

are so often the chorus

in life

but not much heard

as they are not yet of the citizenry

Mz N had a horror

of most groups

though she joined several
which came from a horror of the pressure
of coercion countered by the pressure
of having to think about everything
from the ground up she felt continuously
the iron logic
of what was obvious
yet so perilous
everyone furiously strained
to keep it so
Viz. God
Viz. Family
Viz. Good behavior
Mz N lacked the courage
to smoke
herself out of her covert she tried
to read Nietzsche
but failed what was he saying What
what was he What was he saying
She felt he would answer
to something failed
& instead of reading lived out
the death of god
in her life

The major genres
of modernity are not interested
in this story
& Mz N is often uninterested
isn't this interesting
how the bourgeois individual
was always making himself
against a horizon of love
& work which resolved into
his own projection of a classed grid
a kind of massive erection of the self
amidst the machinery
of institutions—
Well
There are other nodes
Other genres
Other genders
One can be visible
in the world & invisible
One can be a glacier
only the tip of yourself visible
in the open cold blue air

Mz N Enough

Enough with the children
with memory mountain
& bliss was it in that dawn
nostalgia porn
fueling the perpetual infancy
of a glutted citizenry
All the skinny girls
sing *I'm so fat*
they wear their skinny
polemical hats
but O the adults
of Central Europe!
I fell in love
with her sd my friend
in Berlin because
she had no expectations
Soviet bloc austerity
revealed another way
to want. Mz N's thoughts
of others their opacities

only sometimes resolve
into clear expressive skies
when all the people in the world
might suddenly rise
& sing or walk sublimely conversing
a *sacra conversazione*
as in Giovanni di Paolo's *Paradise*
Speech / is a mouth
& a blade
held against the throat
of justice
& a blade of grass
held against the lips
& brightly played
a tone as old
as the mastodons whose bones
enthralled Thomas Jefferson
What is the grass
What is the earth
And may not a reed
be fashioned for us
by us out of this parallel
immaterial world
Should we all swing scythes
like Levin go to scything school

with the just man in England
who reminds his friends
of the work of hands and land
Are we not made of earth
and stars the dust
an old god breathed
into accident
& if I love the green
of green is it green
or all the greens quilted
in the mind I love?
If I say fir and fescue
and clover and lover
whither identity and qualia?
I am I am the iambs
and trochees of assertion wobbling
like Weebles who always
get up as I now do
thanks to you
dear one who's extended
a sweet hand right now
your hand now warm now capable
as hand in hand we take
our provisional
companioned way

II

—N—

Mz N Goodbye Hello / Mz N Considers the Years and the Centuries

Mz N was a kid
for a long time & then
wasn't   Hello
21st century Goodbye
endless adolescence
the old wishes
to be dead
or same thing furious
& alive
& done with the coffin
of youth—
the ones who touch you
and leave no mark
the skin of those years
an unrippled water
anyone could drink from
it always seemed the same
the lake of the self

calm as glass
over years
centuries
you saw
its slow moving

Mz N Monster

So how are you
going to commodify
your brain
asks the mulleted wanker
at the first sherry hour
which features no sherry
and lasts a grim three hours.
The mind fails
& depression acquires a new note
that will sound
instantly in this
our new concerto.

Everyone
it seems
has an archive.
What is an archive
It is a place
of dead things

one can rake over
& decide
if they're still dead.
Mostly they are
or should be.
Frankenstein
is a relevant allegory
and sometimes the very picture
of the real
body made up of salvaged sewn bits.
Mz N has a thing
for monsters
or monster movies at least
She is a secondhand
connoisseur after all
those childhood Saturday afternoons
watching *Monster Movie Matinee*
with the dad
and sometimes the brother.
What's happening
What's happening now
Who's that
the brother asks each time
someone lurches into view
until she tells him

Shut up.
If you can't learn
to pay attention
you'll never understand
how things go
This irks
the brother
who is often outflanked
by Mz N's verbalism
such that he once punched her
wholly deservedly
to shut her up
This was years after
she'd dared him at breakfast
to pour milk over her head
& he did
It wasn't clear
who was more surprised
The skim milk ran down
a watery stream
from the pitcher
It was a pale fluid
It was not blood
or a toxic slime mad scientists
concocted or The Blob

The small angers
of suburbia
here bred nothing
murderous yet
the villagers gathered
with pitchforks
as dumbfounded they plotted
over breakfast
their escape

Mz N Hater

Mz N wants to be like Hazlitt
a great hater
There is so much
to hate   The haters
The mingy minions
of the lesser courts
who attend the chatterati
The fetid fawners
The kissup/kickdown
crapola crew
The given arrangements
called "the world"
But most and first her self
   shame/contempt
   shame/contempt
   systole/diastole of a faulty pump
   i.e. Mz N
If she were true
to "herself"

she would be a hermit
turn isolato
take the narrow road
to the deep North
with Bashō and his tired horse
leave deathless lines
at every bamboo'd stop
catch the words
of whores and kids en route
& the lonely sound of rain
O to take the path
of a hundred weathered bones
and nine orifices
to take a pseudonym
under a banana tree
to travel true
anonymous as a variable
under the sign
of an adopted tree
one carries invisible on a bent back
A windswept spirit finally open
to whatever

Mz N Hermit

And now a hermit thrush
the monster never heard
nor Frankenstein nor Keats
nor Mz N till this moment
Where are the songs
of spring Ay where &
What are the songs
of your climate
Let's ring the changes
of the changing songs
    Did you steep too long
in the tea of your wrongs
Did you break your mind
on hard rocks of thought
Did you find in old poets
an ocean for swimming
or drowning
And what am I
that I should linger here
Mz N wonders

when considering
no longer lingering
on this old earth
          Let's say a hermit thrush
says fuck all but still
it's nice to hear on Bastille Day
the revolution sends its flares
still up   *Far and near*
Did many a heart in Europe
leap to hear
That faith and tyranny
were trampled down
As if   In retrospect
you can sort it all out
In the moment it's fuzzy

Is that an alibi

Isn't it always clear
who the tyrants are
Everyone feels the tyrant
is someone else or necessary
Let's shock the corpse
of the necessary   Shock ourselves
into the unthought possible
My aspiration in life

would be to be happy
says Beyoncé   O life
liberty the pursuit of pursuit of
Let's not talk about Coleridge
and sadness   Let's not talk
about Virginia Woolf
and madness or Lord Byron's
badness or Shelley's drowned
& burnt heart   Mary Shelley wrote
prodigiously   Pampered
her insipid surviving son
What should we do
Après le déluge
Victor left Geneva
Alien now alien in his natal home
The Monster would have left
for South America with his mate
but for her murder & his ice rage
Mary and Shelley left
for France with Claire
Then they left for Italy
Keats left for Italy
Wordsworth left for France
Dorothy and Wordsworth and Coleridge
left for Germany   Burns
would have left for Jamaica

Wordsworth left the Lakes
then never left
but for a tour in Scotland
Scott never left
but to scrounge souvenirs
from the battlefield
of Waterloo   Southey would have left
for the Susquehanna with Coleridge
Coleridge left for Malta
Byron left for the Continent
Blake every day left
this merely empirical earth
Clare could never leave
the fields he saw
enclosed ill-used his mind
cracking along the fissures
of a broken estate   Clare left
for the asylum and left
the asylum and sometimes Clare left
his mind   They all left
for death   the "lost treasure"
of revolutions   left
abandoned or bestowed
—*sovran voices, agonies,*
Creations and destroyings,
all at once / Pour

into the wide hollows of my brain—
They grow in her
They replace her head
with electrified thought
her veins now full
with blood they bled
Then what is life
in the early nineteenth century
in the late twentieth century
in Dante's Italy
in a Midwestern city
Then what is life?
I cried reading old Shelley
but ah Mz N untethered
to the real   balloon adrift
in vacant clouds   Who
do you think you are
—Solitary the thrush,
The hermit withdrawn
to herself, avoiding
the settlements of adulthood
—the Poet's self-centred
seclusion was avenged by the furies
of an irresistible passion
pursuing her to speedy ruin

Mz N Woman

One day Mz N meets a woman
slightly horsefaced
hair a tangle
strong teeth and features
eyes black pools
Who knew this
was beauty
Not Mz N
Not yet
Eros is a hard god
Eros is sly
It is always the case
Mz N never feels the arrow
right away
It takes days
months years then
where that arrow hit
BANG O Now

O Now Mz N Doth Feel It
So hard to align
the when & then
Jetztzeit of the stricken moment
for she was eternal stricken
knew it
by a dream
when making love with X
she woke and
O
not this not O
& there
unavoidable now
the new mouth
she'd move through
this new thing
new tongue new lungs
suckerpunched sucker
dread delight
O Sappho what do you want this time
A revelation can be violent
the tearing the rending
of the veil aletheia
the truth of the soul

lurching for what it wants
cunt a pulse
and most the tube
of the chest blown through
the body all instrument
for this new breathing

Mz N Song

I caught that arrow
you meant for me
and dipped its tip
in blackest ink
and wrote you out

Mz N River Interval

This is my river
of nothing. No one
steps here twice
& most drown in the rush
of its whitewatered ongoingness
unforgiving but beautiful
as the idea of Athens
whitely and dispassionately just.
Those that have the power
to hurt and will do none
look into the eyes
& see nothing
of themselves and thus you cry
certain of a new night
you'll not recover from.
Death metal.
Swarm the dark waters.
The burst beat
is the beat burst the banks

burst the beat
the drums bursting
the ear bursting riverdrums
in bursts of nothing
as nothing bursts

Mz N Thirteenth Floor

Let's say he lives
on the thirteenth floor
which exists despite superstition
and the hookers hang
in the foyer mingling
with the more or less
respectable not that they
don't of course deserve etcetera
An apartment by the lake
If this were the '50s
it would be a pad
a bachelor pad all Frank
and martinis and swank
It has that vibe
though it's not the '50s
and he's not Ol' Blue Eyes
though he has blue eyes
He's an explorer
of sensation ethnographer

videographer of the real
He is muy curioso
and concedes a tendency
toward nostalgia
regarding other lives
he might have lived   What ho
In this one life
to live stay tuned
at 11:00 he's directing
an episode starring
though she doesn't know it
Mz N who seems up
more or less for anything
though maybe it's just
she's apathetic
So hard to distinguish
the oh sure from whatever
She doesn't talk
He doesn't ask
It seems intrusive
Language a late
mammalian acquisition
Why not stick
to the gestural now
He is nothing

if not not intrusive
He's debonair his savoir faire
a thing raw
Americans lack.
He has a reputation
as an excellent lover
conveyed by an ex-lover
a potential lover of Mz N
O roundelay
O lurch & sway
& dip & swing
He's adept at partnering
with a mellow almost joie
de vivre if joie were leavened
by a sharp observing
and self-remembering
In his silent way
he's observing
how she'll accept
this latest role in the latest play
Location: his bedroom
Prop: saran wrap
Prop: duct tape
Prop: bed
Direction: wrap him

Blocking: he tells her
to stand there & wrap him
Wrap him head to toe
He is in his bedroom
naked he commands her
wrap him
head to toe
& then implicitly
fuck him
& bemused she obeys
Well what is this
Well who could say
One supposes it heightens
sensation O strap O leather
O rubber O latex of dungeon
masks of the focalized
sensorium now
O deprivation
you rev my motorcar
you take me oh you take me oh so far
Is that Pat Metheny
on the turntable
was that a bottle
of wellchosen red
did it make

for an interesting
night? She follows through
but he can't help
thinking her
a disappointment
Why can't she embrace
the occasion initiate
an action   Everything
he has to do everything
just like the guy
who wanted to fuck Mz N
's friend up the ass
but she was eh
she was not so into it not least
because she wasn't into him
so why give up her ass
even out of curiosity
Why is everything a giving
up a giving up your X or Y
I'd be promiscuous
if I weren't so contemptuous
this friend told Mz N one night
Uh huh
Everybody
has a thing

they really want
and no one will give it to them
& that's the thing they want
Desire
is endless
disappointment
Desire is lack
blah blah blah
Is this true is it
an endlessly renewed
box of crayons
all gone gray
The gray scale
of her sensuality
is dampening his jouissance recipe
the coño bomb he wants to set off
between her breasts defused
smooth jazz all the way

Mz N Trans

Mz N has met
her first transgender person
though she doesn't know it
yet. She knows Jack.
Jack is her best friend
Val's partner.
Val studies gender.
It seems impossible
not to study gender.
Mz N likes Jack
well enough he seems
laconic typical
guy. Mz N is full
of stereotypes
despite vigilance
They help her
get through
After seven years
Jack tells Val

he wants to be
a woman, wants
to be in fact
although he doesn't say it
Val.
Val was brave
Val was game
She was a heroine
Jack was a heroine
Everyone is the heroine
of her own story
There the hero goes
assuming the world
awaits her
What is a plot
What is reversal
What is recognition
What is the genre
of gender
Jack's speech undid Val
not because Jack
wanted to become Jill
was in fact Jill
though the gods
fucked that up

The new gods
hormones electrolysis
voice coaching
and if need be
the deft surgeons
could fix that
All could be fixed!
Val could have met
Jill maybe loved Jill
as Jill if she hadn't known Jack
just as Jack
a Jack who'd given no inkling
of jokers in the pack
Did I mention
Val studied gender?
So did Jack
who after some time
became Jill
in a wild rush
of becoming that seemed to Jill
an answering
of every errant prayer
Now when Jill's sad
as she sometimes is
she cannot be sad as Jack

Jack's gone
though he left his mark
It would have been better
for me if you'd died
Val found herself
saying. Mz N
thought she understood
How could the beloved
undo the beloved
body? He had a skin
under his skin
in her skin for so long
How could one
not know for so long?
Jack was sorry
but she had to be Jill
in a hurry
Amazing
how many fires flare
in the space
of a single life
Amazing
how we want others
to go with us
just the way we want them to

Jack and Jill went up the hill
Fetch the pail
Fetch the pail
of water, all
There's more to this
than ashes

Mz N Therapy

Mz N has a friend
who is who's dying
Hello friend
Don't die
Don't prove
yet again
the omnipotence of thoughts
a lie
I command you
live!   Thus Mz N commanded
her friend
who is now dead
She was
in the first instance
to Mz N
a voice
on the phone and after
that interview and another
in person
her therapist

Mz N was a case
of extremity
thus therapy
enabled by health insurance
and a state
of emergency
and Illinois and a university
Sometimes Mz N loves
the state
wants to pay more taxes
pledge allegiance fill out a census every day
then lapses her whole life
a lapse & no felix
culpa why was she
all to-torne
as in Chaucer
why was she
so friendly
with her local abyss
that to her was global

Well
There are things
one could say about that
and the therapist did
but mainly let Mz N spool out
what she needed to

the enormous coil the tangled innards
One could spin the thread
into any number of fabrics
designs or fates or snip them
Mz N had never gone
to therapy
it wasn't in the family
repertoire and somewhere
deep within she knew
if she went she'd shatter
She was shattered
so she went
all the billion shards
of her held in a cup
in Chicago by the lake
a great blue lake
that seemed the unblinking eye
of a cold alien god
There was nothing
not worth talking about
not worth being quiet about
How interesting silences
How interesting the little rages
upsurging
for years
this woman

who was mainly a voice
a tall presence
with stupendous breasts foregrounded
surely by whatever stage
of regression Mz N was then in
This is such an old hermeneutic
it stinks of the '90s
the 1890s and cocaine and hysteria
& fin-de-siècle inquiry
and that is where she had to be
in the late 20th century
Mz N was always belated
to herself
as one is
It is so hard
to be contemporary
especially with oneself
always living forward thinking
backward Hello
Present Tense

Because she was paying
to have a dreamlife she had one
filled with terrors and clichés
& she wrote them her dreams down
acquiring a stunning facility
in waking recall

or was it invention

O doubt

O neurosis

Those days

Mz N was closer

to psychosis

stayed clear

perhaps stupidly

of the brainsoothing drugs

which would

her friends told her

put a floor under her

She wasn't walking

She was flying

a grinning demon

in Bosch a lurid hell

of florid-colored pains

My mind to me

a torment is

I am *both a burden and a terror*

to myself

she sd and dreamed

her first official therapy dream

featuring Gertrude Stein

& a cigar which struck her

as rather obvious

There was no way to think
about everything feel it all
out from the ground of being
up. Sometimes
you just have to go
with it
She was
she admitted
stuck
stuck in a crashed plane
she dreamed her friend
might open a door
from   O would she   would she
She awoke
The therapist was patient
glamorous engaging
& yet not usually
intrusive
which was a plus
People are stupid
and mediocre
years later she sd
reflecting on the human condition
brought home to her by her death sentence
It is still possible
for genius

to go unrecognized
in America
Mz N knows it
She knows her friend a genius
who's dead.
What is a genius
A genius channels the spirit
of original
creation singularly
Or, *To believe*
your own thought, to believe
that what is true for you
in your private heart is true
for all—
that is genius
A genius
usually has to make something
and if you just are
if you just privately exist
then you can go missing
as a genius
Talents untried
are talents unknown.
I should have shown myself
more in the world

she said
then died
What is waste
What is loss
Therapy
was the worst experience
of Mz N's life
except for those experiences
which brought her to therapy.
It was arduous
an ordeal a test a trial
agon acid bath
of introspection
& co-feeling barely held
together in the cup of the room
Strange soul techne
peculiar praxis the Vale
of Soul-Making had come
to this O Thel
running from the Vale of Har
stay put stay where you are—

Fare forward woman
wherever the eternal are

Mz N Baby

One day her sister
asked Mz N
to have her baby
This was intriguing
this was frightening
as there had been no babies
come thru her
& to have a baby
not her baby
seemed a strong hard thing
to split the body for.
Shitting
a pumpkin
is what a friend
of Shulamith Firestone
said in the late '60s
it was like
This birth thing
This birthing

The midwives
were gathering
a sharp-eyed coven prepared
to elbow out
the doctors who after all
have long done harm
as much as not.
Mz N's sister
didn't quite ask her
It was more a raising
of the question.
All that summer
she thought
along a country road
about this thing.
Not to the future
but the fuchsia
she thought eyeing
the dicentra and misremembering
Gertrude Stein.

Not the past
but the last possible thing
Isn't it strange to think
I have a dick
in me the pregnant teen said

to her dismayed dad
in a short story.
More stories
these days embrace babies.
Before
they were there
more as ghost cries.
There he goes crowing
sd Gertrude Stein
of Hemingway
about the birth of his son
as if a million men
every day
weren't fathers.
She had a point
but still.
That little baby
is Bumby
in *A Moveable Feast*.
There was nothing
more romantic
than the way
Hem and his wife
shared a bottle of wine
in their bare cabin

in the winter woods
I used to think.
The whole book
seemed a valentine
from another time.
He sd they were poor
& repeated it
but I didn't believe it.
That baby grew up
& did not kill himself
unlike his father and grandfather.
Babies
are romantic
if they are subordinate.
The minute
they rise up all scream
it's a new wound.
Why not let yourself
be torn?
Why not let anything
be born?
Mz N wondered
how anyone
ever made a decision
especially women.

Reason

is but choosing

but there are so many reasons.

Choice

is a fallacy

sustained by the ideology

of the individual

says a friend of Mz N.

Nevertheless.

The thrush

doesn't choose to sing

but sings

& the maple

can't choose not to leaf out

& Mz N can't choose

not to drift

through a summer of possibles

& unresolved doubts

Mz N Calling

It takes a long while
to grow a body
some burst into the world
all flesh and stretch
and the glory of athletes
is theirs
Mz N acquired a body
like the British some say
acquired an empire
in a fit of absence of mind
What were the changes
The terrible mutinies
The suppressions
the nips the blood
the swelling O say

Say there is a woman
her voice a calling
she doesn't know

she's the source of
She's a vehicle
for what for what
for Mz N's falling
Let's not press the world
into yr ego shape
Let's let what falls
fall straight off the table
to the floor you're lying on
listening to a new symphony
drowning your mind
in Górecki's deep wave
Symphonies
are romantic oceanic
All these metaphors
have a dark birth
in the real
Mz N is falling
falls fell is fallen
I fall // you fall // he she or it falls
This is a simple conjugation
and her sentence

Mz N What

what to call
what we did
last night

Mz N Abyme

What
is an orgasm
It is a spasm
of more or less
intense pleasure
a discharge
Freud said
of an intolerable buildup
of tension which evolution
has conditioned us
to experience as pleasure
It is associated
with sex
more often in men

Desire
is not a thing
it is an irresistible humming vibrating
through the body

all present tense
as the surge
explodes what you thought
was yr skin

Sometimes
Mz N just wants
to ride
that thing
human being
filling up
her every crack
& making
itself heard
through her
an open
mouth.
You
are that thing
can't but
secrete it.
Your secret
gaps untouched
in a known
world the tiny spheres

of something
no one knows
how/to say
All that emptiness
fuller
than yr eventual
dust. Every crevice
in the atom a space
where nothing happens
but could

A congeries
of possibles

The space between the geese
now moving in the sky

Mz N Love Lies Sleeping / Moon

There is a long debate
among the philosophers
of love do you love
the beloved or her qualities
It's clear Mz N loves
the beloved asleep
right now in the swart tent
they set out in the night
in the moon's slow rising
in love's remembering
With how sad steps
the moon has climbed
the skies & with glad steps
it now arises mounts
the sky and hangs above
an old mountain.
If the owl and the pussycat
went to sea in a beautiful
pea-green boat & if love

quotes Edward Lear
she is more dear
but not the beloved
for that. The Elizabethans
got it wrong
with their endlessly inventive
and reiterative blazons
itemizing love as if
love were a rhetorical series
contained in a little song
and not the thrust push
& lull of song going
on and on and on
as if love's plum lips
hips and breasts
long thighs and singularly arched
brows lakeblue eyes
the golden zone the swell
and all & praised
could ever start to raise
the sail on the boat
now setting forth
on a moonlit pond

Mz N Meadow

Somewhere after wildness
a meadow
is good for dreaming
and crickets
and remembering the word
for grasshopper
in French.
We have put down
our tankards
We do not smash
the boards in a meadhall
Our armor unlike ants'
is wholly inside
our bodies
The skin of a meadow
is grass
and wildflowers who return

as if invited
by the season to visit
a long unbroken field
to accept the hospitality
of the why not hello

Mz N Palinode

Just like you
to sing a flower song
of love   ignore
the lash of labor
you're not under

Just like you
to lean on a lyre
float in a meadow
when the cracking world
needs action, facts

Just like you
to set a course
then lose yourself
in Siren's siren

your little privacies
now whirling

down the pool
of something else required

Did you not think
the world larger

Are the old songs
all wrong

In her next life
Mz N will be serious
and public and save
the republic
turn singularity
into solidarity
or retreat
into a silence
proper to a chaos
that eludes any kiss
or word of a kiss

—N—

Envoi / N-Voi

Enervated Endymion endures, encants, energizes
enthralled engineers.

Endorse endorphins, endocrinologists.

Engender enchanters, engineers.

Enervate enemies, enclose entropy.
Ensnare envious envoys. Enjamb
enjambment.

Enable encounters.
Ensure enquiry.
Entertain entelechy.

Encourage. Enjoy. Enlarge energy.

Enter entirely.

Ensorcell entities.

Entwine. Enamor. Enrage. Engage. Endure.

§

End N.

Acknowledgments

I am grateful to the editors and publishers of the following journals, in which some episodes of this book first appeared: *The American Scholar*, *Blackbox Manifold*, *Granta*, *Literary Hub*, *London Review of Books*, *The Paris Review*, *Prac Crit*.

For their support during the writing of this project, deepest thanks to Blue Mountain Center, the Corporation of Yaddo, the MacDowell Colony, and the New York University Global Research Initiative. I am grateful to these institutions and the provisional communities and enduring friendships they sponsored: energizers.

Thanks as well to Jeff Clark (again!): envisioner; and to Jo Stewart: ensurer.

To Yvonne Rainer: enjamber; and to Vicki Olwell: camarada.

Thanks to Ellen Eisenman, who early on wanted more; August Kleinzahler, who knows wherefore; Robyn Creswell, who read and more; Rachael Allen, Adam Fitzgerald, Langdon Hammer, Cathy Park Hong, Alex Houen, Sarah Howe, Luke Neima, and especially Jonathan Galassi, who asked: encouragers.

For my teachers, dead and alive, human and not.

For my parents, who chose Noelle.

For L: enamoring *elle*.